THE SEVEN PRAYERS OF FÁTIMA
IN LATIN AND ENGLISH

THE SEVEN PRAYERS OF FÁTIMA
IN LATIN AND ENGLISH

Edited by
Geoffrey W.M.P. Lopes da Silva

DOMINA NOSTRA PUBLISHING
Monterey, California, USA

Published in 2021 by
Domina Nostra Publishing, Inc.
P.O. Box 1464, Monterey, CA. 93942-1464 USA
Email: info@DominaNostraPublishing.com
Website: www.DominaNostraPublishing.com

Copyright © 2021 Domina Nostra Publishing, Inc.

Printed and bound in the United States of America.
All rights reserved.

Latin texts of the Fatima Prayers are taken from *Preces a B.V. Maria in Apparitionibus Fatimae factis vel ab Angelo adulescentulis,* Editiones Familiae Sancti Hieronymi. Copyright © 1991.

English texts of the Fatima Prayers are adapted from *Our Lady of Fátima*, by William T. Walsh, the MacMillan Company, 1947 and *Fatima in Lucia's Own Words: Sister Lucia's Memoirs*, 9th edition (1995), edited by Rev. Louis Kondor, SVD.

Although the editor and publisher have made every effort to ensure the accuracy and completeness of information contained in this book, we assume no responsibility for errors, inaccuracies, omissions, or any inconsistency herein. Any slights of people, places, or organizations are unintentional, and will be corrected in the next edition.

ISBN: 978-0-9741900-5-1

First printing, 2021

"At a time when the human family was ready to sacrifice all that was most sacred on the altar of the petty and selfish interests of nations, races, ideologies, groups, and individuals, our Blessed Mother came from heaven, offering to implant in the hearts of all those who trust in her the Love of God burning in her own heart".

Pope Benedict XVI
Homily at Fátima in Portugal
13 May 2010

Introduction

The Prayers of Fátima (*Orationes Fatimæ*) are seven prayers that originated before, during, and after the apparitions of the Blessed Virgin Mary at Fátima, Portugal in 1917. The apparitions were deemed "worthy of belief" on 13 October 1930 by Dom José Alves Correia da Silva, the twenty-second Bishop of Leiria.

In 1916, just prior to the apparitions of Our Lady of the Holy Rosary of Fátima, an angel appeared to the Servant of God Maria Lúcia of Jesus and of the Immaculate Heart née Lúcia de Jesus Rosa dos Santos (1907-2005) and her cousins Saint Francisco de Jesus Marto (1908-1919) and Saint Jacinta de Jesus Marto (1910-1920). The angel called himself the *Anjo da Guarda de Portugal*, Portuguese for "Guardian Angel of Portugal".

The angel, who has also been referred to as the Custodian Angel (*Anjo Custódio*) and the Angel of Peace (*Anjo da Paz*), taught the three shepherd children the **Pardon Prayer (*oratio veniæ*)** in the spring of 1916 and the **Angel's Prayer (*oratio angeli*)** in the autumn of 1916. When teaching the three seers the latter prayer, they saw a vision of the Most Blessed Sacrament suspended in the air before which the Holy Guardian Angel of Portugal prostrated himself and prayed this **Act of Reparation to the Most Holy Trinity**.

On 13 May 1917, the Blessed Virgin Mary appeared for the first time. In addition to telling the three seers the importance of praying the Rosary, she also asked the three children if they would be willing to offer sacrifices in reparation for the sins of the world.

After the three children agreed, the Holy Virgin then said: "You will have much to suffer, but the grace of God will be your comfort". At the words "the grace of God", the Holy Virgin held out her hands and the three children experienced a great light surrounding and penetrating them. Without thinking about it, they found themselves praying the **Eucharistic Prayer (*oratio eucharistica*)**, no doubt under the inspiration of the Holy Spirit.

During the apparition of 13 June 1917, the Blessed Virgin taught the **Decade Prayer (*oratio decadis*)** and the **Sacrifice Prayer (*oratio sacrificii*)** to the three seers. The Decade Prayer is also known as "the Fátima Prayer" because it is the most commonly known of the Seven Prayers of Fátima. It is added at the end of each decade of the Rosary, immediately following the Minor Doxology (*doxologia minor*) or Glory to the Father (*Gloria Patri*). The Sacrifice Prayer is said when offering up an action or some suffering in a spirit of sacrifice. This prayer, spoken sincerely, effectively allows any hardship, illness, or pain in one's life to be offered as acts of reparation. *Nota bene:* The words that appear in parentheses were added at a later date.

The **Conversion Prayer (*oratio conversionis*)** and the **Salvation Prayer (*oratio salvationis*)** were taught to the last of the living seers, the Servant of God Lúcia dos Santos by Christ Himself in August of 1931. He asked her to pray for the conversion and salvation of the world through the Immaculate Heart of Mary. Even though these two prayers did not come to existence in Fátima but rather in Rianjo, Spain after the Servant of God had entered the Institute of the Sisters of Saint Dorothy in 1925, they are nevertheless classified as "Fátima Prayers".

Septem Orationes Fatimæ

1 ORATIO VENIÆ

Deus meus,
in te credo, te adóro, tibi confído, te amo!
Pro illis qui non credent,
non adórant, non confident,
et non amant véniam supplico.

2 ORATIO ANGELI
(ACTUS REPARATIONIS AD SANCTISSIMAM TRINITATEM)

Sanctíssima Trinitas,
Pater, Fílius et Spíritus Sanctus,
profunde te adóro;
tibi óffero pretiosissimum corpus, sánguinem,
ánimam et divinitátem Iesu Christi
præséntem in totis tabernaculis mundi
in reparatione contumeliarum, sacrilegiorum,
et neglegentiarum, quibus offenditur.
Per infiníta merita
Sacratissimi Cordis Iesu
et Immaculátæ Cordis Maríæ
conversiónem peccatórum peto.

The Seven Prayers of Fátima

1 THE PARDON PRAYER

My God,
I believe, I adore, I hope, and I love You!
I ask pardon of You for those who do not believe,
do not adore, do not hope,
and do not love You.

2 THE ANGEL'S PRAYER
(ACT OF REPARATION TO THE MOST HOLY TRINITY)

Most Holy Trinity,
Father, Son, and Holy Spirit,
I adore You profoundly,
and I offer You the most precious Body, Blood,
Soul, and Divinity of Jesus Christ,
present in all the tabernacles of the world,
in reparation for the outrages, sacrileges,
and indifference with which He Himself is offended.
And, through the infinite merits
of the Most Sacred Heart of Jesus
and of the Immaculate Heart of Mary
I beg of You the conversion of poor sinners.

*"Make of everything you can a sacrifice,
and offer it to God as an act of reparation
for the sins by which He is offended,
and in supplication for the conversion of sinners".*

The Guardian Angel of Portugal
1916

3 ORATIO EUCHARISTICA

Sanctíssima Trinitas, te adóro!
Deus meus, Deus meus,
te amo in Sanctissimo Sacraménto.

4 ORATIO SACRIFICII

O Iesu, est propter amórem tui,
et conversiónem peccatórum,
et in reparatione peccatórum
contra cor Maríæ Immaculátum commissorum
(ut orem).

5 ORATIO DECADIS (ORATIO FATIMA)[1]

O mi Iesu, dimítte nobis débita nostra,
líbera nos ab igne inférni,
conduc in cælum ómnes ánimas,
præsertim illas, quæ máxime indigent
(misericórdia tua).

---

[1] *Alternate Latin translation:*

Dómine Iesu, dimítte nobis debíta nostra, salva nos ab igne inferiori, perduc in cælum ómnes ánimas, præsertim eas, quæ misericórdiæ tuæ máxime indigent.

Or:

Mi Iésu, indúlge peccáta nóstra, consérva nos ab ígne inférni, duc ómnes ad cáeli glóriam, præcípue túa misericórdia egéntes.

3 THE EUCHARISTIC PRAYER

O Most Holy Trinity, I adore You!
My God, my God,
I love You in the Most Blessed Sacrament.

4 THE SACRIFICE PRAYER

O Jesus, it is for the love of You,
in reparation for the offences committed
against the Immaculate Heart of Mary,
and for the conversion of poor sinners
(that I pray / do this).

5 THE DECADE PRAYER (THE FATIMA PRAYER)

O my Jesus, forgive us of our sins.
Save us from the fires of hell.
Lead all souls into heaven,
especially those in most need
(of Thy mercy).

*"My Immaculate Heart will be your refuge
and the way that will lead you to God".*

Our Lady of Fátima
13 June 1917

*"In the end, my Immaculate Heart will triumph…
In Portugal, the dogma of the Faith
will always be preserved…"*

Our Lady of Fátima
13 July 1917

6 ORATIO CONVERSIONIS

Conceptióne tua pura et immaculáta,
  O María,
conversiónem Russiæ, Hispaniæ,
  Lusitaniæ, Europæ
et totíus mundi exora.

7 ORATIO SALVATIONIS

Cor dulce Maríæ,
salvátio sis Russiæ, Hispaniæ,
Lusitaniæ, Europæ, et totíus mundi.

6 THE CONVERSION PRAYER

By your pure and Immaculate Conception,
 O Mary,
obtain the conversion of Russia, Spain,
 Portugal, Europe
and the whole world!

7 THE SALVATION PRAYER

Sweet Heart of Mary,
be the salvation of Russia, Spain,
Portugal, Europe and the whole world.

*"You please Me very much
by praying for the conversion of those countries.
Ask this grace also of My Mother."*

Christ Jesus
August 1931

The Seven Fátima Prayers in Latin and English

"Have compassion on the Heart
of your most holy Mother, covered with thorns,
with which ungrateful men pierce it at every moment,
and there is no one to make an act of reparation
to remove them".

The Christ Child
to the Servant of God Lúcia dos Santos

The Five First Saturdays

In her third apparition at Fátima on 13 July 1917, the Blessed Virgin Mary first mentioned the Five First Saturday devotion, saying: "I come to ask… the Communion of reparation on the first Saturdays". Our Lady of Fátima went into greater detail over eight years later on 10 December 1925, when she and the Christ Child appeared to the Servant of God Lúcia dos Santos in her convent at Pontevedra in Portugal, saying:

> *I promise to assist at the hour of death, with the graces necessary for salvation, all those who, on the first Saturday of five consecutive months,*
> **(1)** *shall confess,*
> **(2)** *receive Holy Communion,*
> **(3)** *recite five decades of the Rosary, and*
> **(4)** *keep me company for fifteen minutes while meditation on the fifteen mysteries of the Rosary, with the intention of making reparation to me.*

On 5 February 1926, the Child Jesus appeared to the Servant of God Lúcia dos Santos to ask if she had spread this devotion. During this apparition, the Servant of God asked the Divine Infant if it might be valid for the faithful to go to Confession within eight days of the First Saturday, as it may be difficult for some to go to Confession on Saturday. The Christ Child replied:

> *Yes, and it could be longer still, provided that, when they receive Me, they are in the state of grace and have the intention of making reparation to the Immaculate Heart of Mary.*

Domina Nostra Publishing

P.O. Box 1464
Monterey, CA. 93942-1464
USA

info@DominaNostraPublishing.com
www.DominaNostraPublishing.com

www.ingramcontent.com/pod-product-compliance
Lightning Source LLC
Chambersburg PA
CBHW062107290426
44110CB00022B/2743